*Gabriola:* PETROGLYPH ISLAND

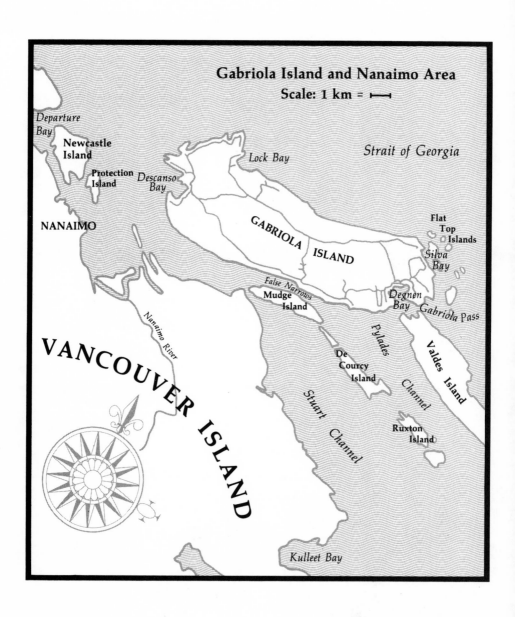

Gabriola Island and Nanaimo Area

Scale: 1 km = ⊢———⊣

Departure Bay

Newcastle Island

Protection Island

Descanso Bay

Lock Bay

Strait of Georgia

NANAIMO

GABRIOLA ISLAND

Flat Top Islands

Silva Bay

Nanaimo River

False Narrows

Mudge Island

Degnen Bay

Gabriola Pass

VANCOUVER ISLAND

De Courcy Island

Pylades Channel

Valdes Island

Stuart Channel

Ruxton Island

Kulleet Bay

# *Gabriola*

# PETROGLYPH ISLAND

## Mary and Ted Bentley

1981

Sono Nis Press

1745 Blanshard Street, Victoria, British Columbia, Canada

Copyright © 1981 by Mary and Ted Bentley.

Canadian Cataloguing in Publication Data

Bentley, Mary.
    Gabriola

        Bibliography: p.
        Includes index.
        ISBN 0-919462-81-2

        1. Petroglyphs—British Columbia—Gabriola Island.
    2. Indians of North America—British Columbia—
    Gabriola Island—Antiquities.
    I. Bentley, Ted. II. Title.

E78.B9B45        732'.23'0971134        C81-091168-X

First Printing June 1981
Second Printing January 1982

The publication of this book would not have been possible
without the assistance of the Canada Council.

COVER PHOTOGRAPH

Could glyphs such as this have been carved to greet
and honour the salmon people at each high tide as
E. L. Keithahn suggests?

Published by
SONO NIS PRESS
1745 Blanshard Street
Victoria, British Columbia

Designed and printed in Canada by
MORRISS PRINTING COMPANY LTD.
Victoria, British Columbia

*Dedicated*
*to*
*Bill*

## *Special thanks to*

British Columbia Heritage Trust

Ethel Bentley

Beth Hill

Mabel and Harold Cliffe

Daniel Leen

Karen Cliffe


All photographs by Ted Bentley unless otherwise stated.
Scale maps and drawings by Mary Bentley

# CONTENTS

View of the Gabriola Weldwood Site from the forested perimeter.

*In the depths of man's mind,*
  *stone is associated with wholeness,*
  *self, truth, and eternity.*

WILSON DUFF
*Images: Stone: B.C.*

# THE CHALLENGE

Pilings creaked and groaned in Descanso Bay as the salt-sprayed *Kahloke* nudged her blunt bow into Gabriola Island's ferry slip. From the van window we impatiently watched a parade of Island residents and visitors trudge slowly up the steep ramp. Circling gulls alighted momentarily to await the ferry's return trip to Nanaimo as we streamed up the narrow roadway.

Our autumn drive down the Island wound past rustling stands of cedar, dogwood and Douglas fir and fields of lethargic sheep enjoying the last warmth of fall sunshine.

Quiet summer homes stared at oystery beaches while an occasional cluster of wind-ruffled black cormorants or a lofty great blue heron perched on barnacled boulders.

Exciting thoughts of new discoveries filled our minds as we turned our van off the meandering Island road and stopped beside a small church in a grassy clearing.

Armed with cotton cloth, black crayons, broom and shovel, we set out. The two children raced ahead while their grandparents and ourselves hesitantly chose an overgrown path which later proved to be a deserted logging road. Brushing aside damp alder branches and carefully stepping over slugs and leaf-strewn puddles, we enthusiastically recalled the information a ferry traveller had casually given mother weeks before, "Oh yes, I saw some carved marks in the sandstone bedrock near the southern road. What do you call these rock carvings—petroglyphs?"

This presented a new challenge to us as amateur archaeologists and fascinated admirers of native Indian culture. Over the previous two years we had recorded and produced cloth rubbings of the five known petroglyphs on Gabriola Island.

Could this musty trail, one of a honeycomb of old logging roads, be the one? Would it lead us to an unrecorded petroglyph site? The persistent, raucous chatter of ravens and crows accompanied our absorbing reflections as we peered from side to side past green sword ferns, salal and wild rose bushes.

It is thought that hundreds of years ago native carvers searched for particular expanses of rock with suggestive shapes, faults and fissures which they believed possessed special power or vitality. Therefore, they often carved many petroglyphs on the same rock face. Some were even superimposed over others, each carving increasing the inherent power of the rock. Which slab of moss-covered sandstone would tempt an ancient rock carver?

After walking down the trail for several minutes we excitedly detected an opening through the salal. Soon a large, secluded clearing encircled by second growth Douglas fir, oak and wild rose came into view.

Burrs clung to our socks and stung our ankles as we hurriedly toured the several acres of sandstone covered with grasses and moss. A strange hush pervaded the enclosure broken only by the rhythmic pecking of a red-shafted flicker re-echoing some ancient stone artist carving a petroglyph with his hammerstone.

Blackberry, wild rose, salal and green sword ferns lined the abandoned logging road.

This 28 cm by 45 cm head and eye, deeply abraded to 5 mm, was one of the Site's visible carvings.

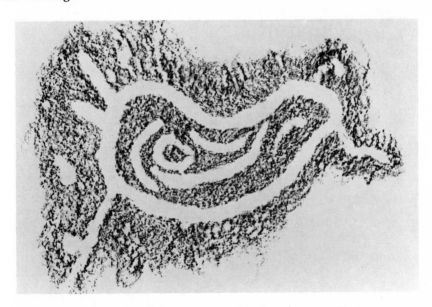

A crayon and cloth rubbing was made of each petroglyph as it was discovered. The white lines correspond with the carved lines on the rock surface.

# THE DISCOVERY

The summer sun, now faded and distant, had baked off patches of moss to expose islands of smooth sandstone. Exploring carefully for a few minutes we discovered one of the Site's visible carvings—undoubtedly the figure which had caught the ferry traveller's eye.

It was an irregular ovoid shape, possibly a head with a central eye. The carving is deeply abraded or smoothed to a depth of 5 mm and has two distinct finger-like projections of uneven lengths at the upper left side.

Did a special power lead us to the rock surface close by where we instinctively rolled back the spongy, wet moss like a thick, green quilt? A deeply carved double eye and head plume of an elaborate petroglyph lay exposed on the glistening bedrock. The root-matted underside of the moss blanket revealed a perfectly embossed, reverse image of the large carving.

Startled and overwhelmed that an Island so familiar should now disclose secrets long hidden, we felt privileged to view this masterfully carved petroglyph for the first time in hundreds of years.

An hour of absorbing and careful work with shovel and broom followed to remove the covering of grass and dirt which deepened on the lower side to 12 cm. A fluidly stylized, mythical creature, 72 cm by 114 cm, was revealed.

To us, the carving is reminiscent of the large-headed, belted kingfisher common in this locale. These crested blue and white birds chatter and scold from arbutus trees then plummet headlong into nearby Degnen Bay and return to their perch with fish.

The Alaskan author, E. L. Keithahn, mentions that local species of birds and animals were often the inspiration for supernatural creatures. Diamond Jenness, in his work, *The Faith of a Coast Salish Indian*, lists the kingfisher as one of the guardian spirits created by "Khaals," a powerful transformer.

In Coast Salish myths the kingfisher was commanded to bestow fishing success on mankind.

We refer to the carving as "kingfisher" although this interpretation is highly subjective and reflects our own Island experience rather than archaeological studies.

The curvilinear lines of the petroglyph design are uniformly, deeply abraded to 5 mm and widened to over 2 cm. No other recorded glyph on the Northwest coast resembles this mythical creature.

Two projections at the tail of the bird identical to those on the nearby ovoid glyph possibly indicate the same rock artist or a similar era of carving. Further sweeping of loose dirt exposed a tiny "crab" petroglyph.

The thrill of discovering the mythical bird would have been sufficient for one day. However, that proved to be only the beginning of our discoveries.

Near the creature's tail we uncovered an enormous, mythical serpent, 1 m by 2.5 m, buried by up to 20 cm of dirt and grass. Like the bird it has deeply carved, 2 cm wide, smoothed lines and has suffered very little erosion.

The serpent is oriented eastward on a rock face which slopes toward a long mound of broken sandstone slabs. The prime placement of these two large carvings on the rock panel suggests that other peripheral glyphs were made at a later date.

The large fin of the serpent, displaying inner structural detail, reflects a typical Northwest coast motif. The entire glyph is remarkably similar to a serpent or dragon-like carving at the Nanaimo River Site (DgRx8).[1]

The serpent's huge double eye and greatly enlarged head are similar to the mythical bird stylistically. Anthropologist, Franz Boas, in *Primitive Art*, noted that head size and facial features were given more emphasis than body and limbs in Northwest coast Indian art.

The serpent, with its enormous mouth, frightening teeth and tongue, and long snake-like body bears a resemblance to the

[1] Borden's petroglyph site numbers.

An elaborate plumed head with double eye lay exposed on the glistening bedrock.

Clayoquot Indians' mythical "Haietlik" mentioned by author, C. F. Newcombe and the "Hahektoak" of Nootkan and Makah legends.

In native myths the Thunderbird flung Haietlik, the Lightening Snake, into the ocean to harpoon whales. Newcombe mentions that several carvings at Nanaimo's Petroglyph Park (DgRx6) and Sproat Lake, Port Alberni (DhSf1), could represent Haietlik. Anthropologist Richard McClure mentions that petro-

A fluidly stylized mythical creature, 72 cm by 114 cm, was revealed.

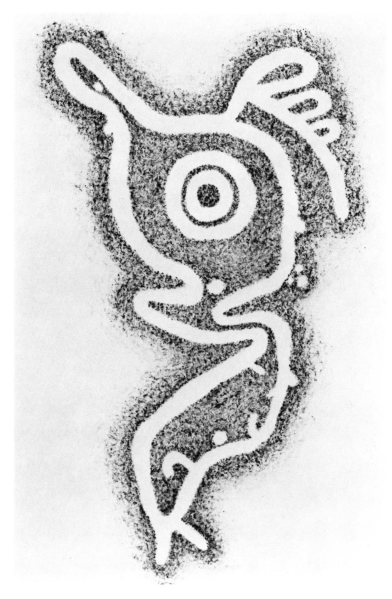

Local species of birds and animals were often the inspiration for supernatural creatures such as this.

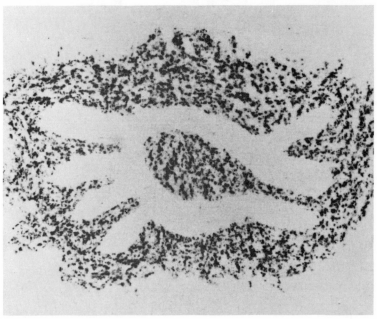

This tiny, pecked crab carving is located at the tail of the bird.

We uncovered an enormous mythical serpent, 1 m by 2.5 m, the same autumn day.

23

The serpent is oriented eastward on a rock face which slopes toward a long mound of broken sandstone slabs.

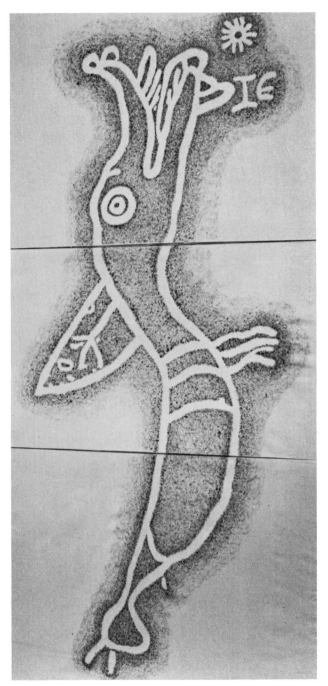

The X-ray style fin and large double eye are typical motifs in Northwest coast Indian art.

The serpent petroglyph could represent the Clayoquot Indians' mythical "Haietlik" or Lightening Snake.

glyphs of Hahektoak carved by Makah whalers may have symbolized a personal guardian spirit quest or have been prominent in whaling ceremonies. Perhaps an individual searching for a guardian or protector carved the serpent after summoning Haietlik's dynamic animal spirit in his hallucinatory visions.

After closely examining this remarkably powerful carving we noticed the same projections from the serpent's tail fluke—identical to those on the ovoid and bird.

Near the mouth of the serpent is a tiny carving of an eleven-rayed sun, perhaps a special symbol intended to increase the serpent's spirit power. A second sun design with eight rays is located east of the serpent. McClure notes that the ray and circle design is a predominant motif in Washington petroglyphs. Other examples of the sun motif appear on the rocks of Chrome Island in British Columbia.

Although the initial thrill of discovery can never be repeated, each visit to the Site throughout the spring and summer of 1977 yielded exciting finds. Always with respect, often with awe, we carefully turned back centuries of moss and dirt to reveal an ancient carved design.

How many years had these incredible carvings remained under grass and moss? Ethel Gray, a retired Gabriola Island resident who lives on nearby property, told us she had played on this Site many times in her childhood. The petroglyph find was as startling to her as it was to other Island pioneers.

The Gabriola Weldwood Site first passed into private hands as a Crown Land Grant in 1887 and was later purchased by Weldwood of Canada Limited. During the Second World War this and other areas of the Island were logged and though there are scratch marks on some of the sandstone from the steel treads of logging equipment, miraculously none of the petroglyphs have suffered permanent damage. The whole Site is now part of a Tree Farm License.

In the fall of 1978 I approached Weldwood of Canada to inform them of the important petroglyph discoveries on their land. The company was fascinated with the find and became immediate supporters of our wish to protect the area. Provincial Archaeologist Bjorn Simonsen later contacted the company and asked for their co-operation in the protection of the Site. Weldwood's response was a generous donation of approximately six hectares (fifteen acres) taking in all the recorded petroglyphs as well as a buffer of trees and access road to the area. Weldwood felt the best way to preserve and protect the Site was to deed the land to the Crown—a commendably positive and supportive action.

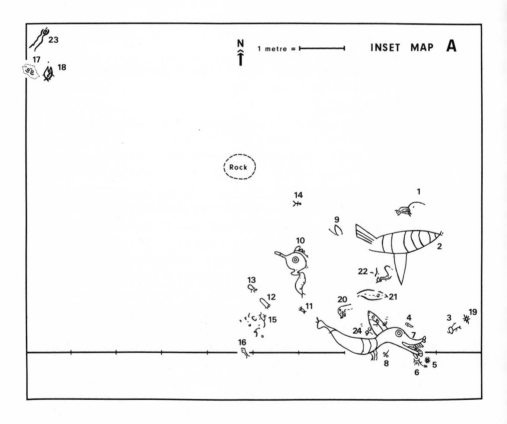

# FURTHER DISCOVERIES

## *Supernatural Beings, Mythical Animals, Symbolic Eyes, Salmon People*

West of the mythical bird six very small glyphs were recorded (Inset Map A). A pair of eyes with brows and nostrils are deeply pecked into a naturally round depression in the rock. This choice of a specific physical location to give a carving dramatic impact exemplifies a widespread rock art tradition. During the winter months the hollow fills with rainwater and the eyes assume a watery glare.

The eye-face motif, one of the most common petroglyph traditions on the Northwest coast and probably one of the oldest, occupied a position of fundamental importance to the shaman or carver. According to Keithahn eyes represented the spirit and essence of some powerful being to be honoured.

Northwest coast eye-faces bear a striking similarity to recorded petroglyphs near the Amur River in Siberia. Anthropologist, Joan Vastokas mentions that this eye-face motif forms part of the *North Pacific Maritime Tradition* (about 3000-2000 B.C.) which extended from coastal Siberia and northern Japan to northern California.

West of the mythical bird a small naturalistic foot can be seen faintly. This pecked, eroded design resembles one at the Nanaimo River Site. The less frequently seen petroglyph footprint and the commonly occurring pictograph handprint may represent a symbolic record of the carver's participation in a ritual experience or his endeavour to receive some of the rock's innate power.

Between the serpent and the original ovoid motif, a large fish, 2 m by 1.3 m, is carved with an eastern orientation. Its angular and narrow line style is in direct contrast to the mythical bird and serpent. The carving seems to be unfinished as the upper

During rainy months the hollow fills with rainwater and the eyes assume a watery glare.

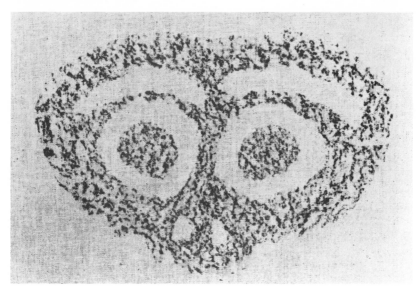

To the carver eyes represented the spirit and essence of some powerful being to be honoured.

The 10 cm by 22 cm foot glyph is an example of an eroded, pecked carving.

One hand of this glaring, oval eyed human rests on a salmon's snout.

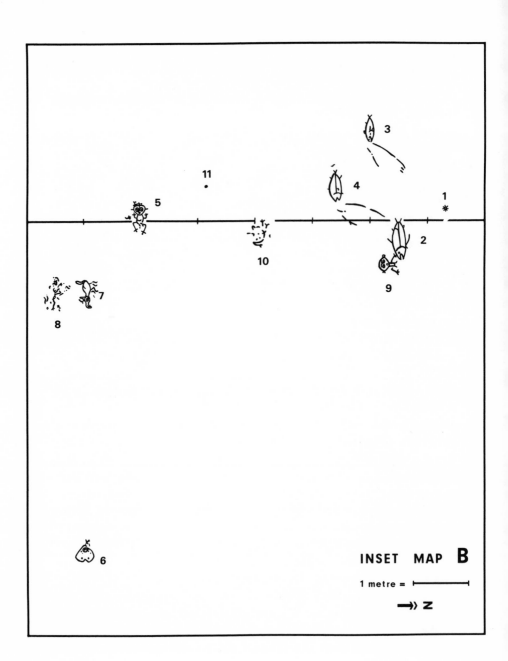

INSET MAP **B**

1 metre = |———————|

➜〉 N

body line ends abruptly and no trace of tail fluke exists. Possibly this fish was begun after the others, on what the carver must have believed was a very power-filled rock face.

The fish design exhibits the ancient X-ray rib style similar to the Jack Point petroglyph boulder. This famous boulder, now located at the Nanaimo Museum, represents in legend the dog salmon who married a shaman's daughter, took her into the sea, and subsequently returned to the Nanaimo River each fall at spawning time.

On a smooth, sloping rock face covered with lichen, three salmon petroglyphs, each pointing eastward, an eight-rayed circle design and a partial humanoid were discovered (Inset Map B). One hand of the glaring, oval eyed human rests on the largest salmon's snout.

These highly eroded, pecked carvings are barely recognizable and difficult to record by photograph or rubbing. The oblique rays of late afternoon sun bring to life a tableau of petroglyphs virtually hidden at any other time of day.

The salmon, whose five species were the mainstay of coastal Indian life, were considered to be special creatures possessing a bodily form and human existence under the sea. According to author Philip Drucker, southern coastal groups believed the salmon people voluntarily transformed themselves into fish as a beneficial offering to man. Therefore, at late summer spawning time, shamans conducted solemn Salmon Rites to honour the "swimmers." Author and artist, Hilary Stewart, mentions that prayers and songs of thanks were offered to the "Supernatural Ones" and prescribed taboos and customs were followed in the harvesting and preparation of the fish. In most native groups the bones of the first catch were reverently returned to the ocean where they were thought to reassemble their human structure and return to their aquatic villages.

South of the salmon glyphs we recorded an eroded, but elegantly fluid carving of a humanoid, highly representative of Northwest coast petroglyph styles. Carved in the smoothed line style, it depicts a man in the usual frontal, frog-like dance position with knees bent and arms turned upward. The large head has a projection or plume radiating from it and the total dimensions are 55 cm by 35 cm.

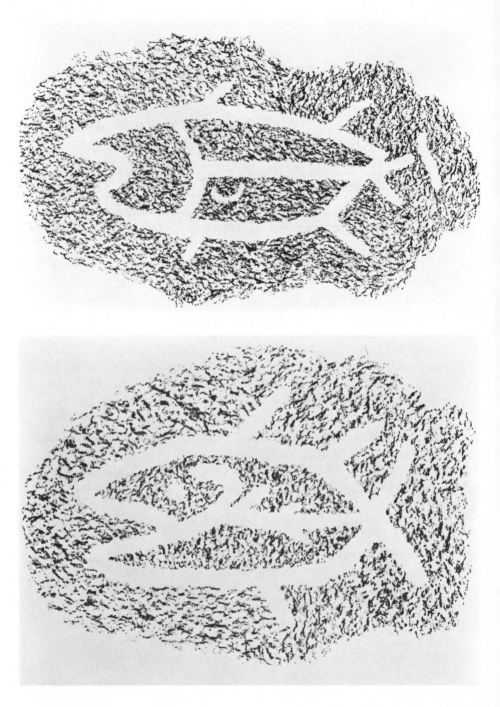

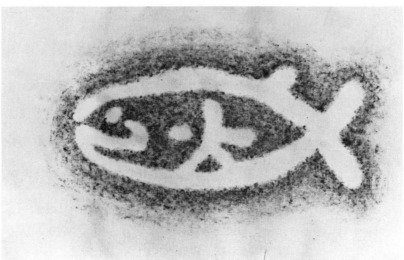

Three highly eroded and indistinct carvings of salmon were discovered
when the long rays of late afternoon sun brought them to life.

This stylistically typical carving depicts a man in the usual frontal, frog-like dance position with knees bent and arms upturned.

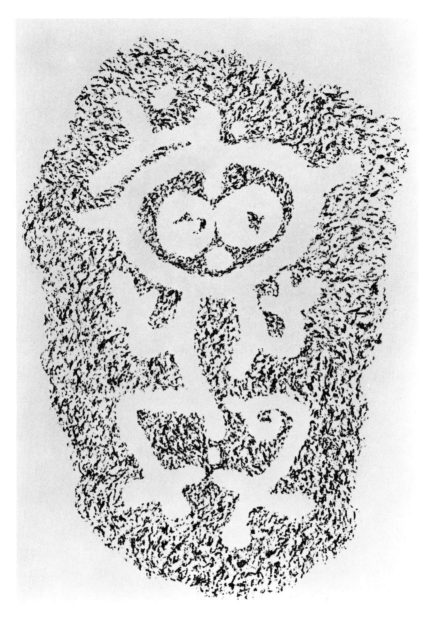

Head plumes or crests distinguish supernatural figures from the ordinary mortal.

This mythical quadruped has oval eyes, a long curved snout and upturned tail.

Keithahn noted that head plumes distinguished supernatural figures from the ordinary mortal. Similarly, Hawaiian authors J. H. Cox and E. Stasack, documented many Hawaiian petroglyph humanoids with crests, loops and arches over their heads.

This stylistic tradition continues today in the contemporary works of Ojibway painter and shaman, Norval Morrisseau, one of the Woodland Indian artists. "Power projections" emanate from his creatures and the X-ray vision style is often evident.

Like the Quadra Island carvings from Cape Mudge (DiSh1) and other anthropomorphic figures found on the Gabriola Weldwood Site, the humanoid's hands and feet are represented by only three digits. Large eyes and animal ears exemplify another stylistic feature and a distinct opening in the figure's right side suggests symbolic significance.

Representations of male genitalia are present in the anthropomorph as in other humanoids discovered at the Site. Beth Hill, in *Indian Petroglyphs of the Pacific Northwest*, reported that greater sexual emphasis was portrayed in Salish and Nootkan rock carvings than in those of more northernly groups.

One of the Site's three mythical quadrupeds is located east of the male figure. This highly eroded animal has oval eyes, a long curved snout and upturned tail.

In April 1979, we unearthed a frightening heart-shaped face east of the humanoid figure. This deep, smoothed line carving, found under 10 cm of grass and dirt, has teeth, penetrating eyes and heavy eyebrows.

In sharp contrast to the curvilinear style of the male figure of Section B is a second humanoid, 50 cm by 40 cm, carved with stick-like angular limbs (Inset Map D). Its lines are a series of pecked holes which have not been abraded into a smooth groove.

A carved depression below the humanoid's mouth may represent a labret. This T-shaped bone or stone decoration was usually worn in the lower lip by young girls, women, and less often, men, as a sign of special status or beauty. According to Hill, a 1973 provincial excavation on a shell midden site on Saltspring Island produced six Coast Salish labrets which were dated to the Marpole Phase (about 500 B.C. to A.D. 500). It is conceivable the rock carvings were executed during this time span

This small, pecked anthropomorph is 40 cm by 50 cm.

A carved depression below the humanoid's mouth may represent a labret.

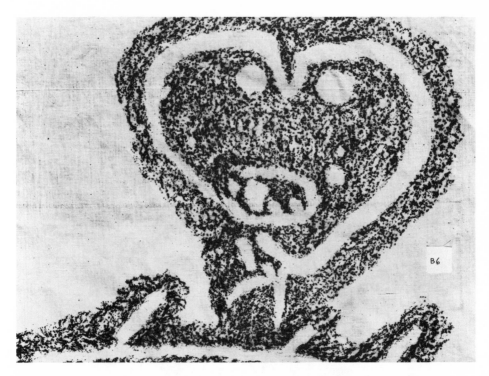

This deeply carved, heart-shaped face has teeth, penetrating eyes and heavy eyebrows. It is 32 cm by 40 cm.

as there is no evidence that labrets were worn in later periods by the Coast Salish.

Near the stick man a faintly abraded head and body was found under a thin layer of soil and a rotting log. This gracefully outlined figure lacks all facial and body detail.

Directly below is a simple, pecked anthropomorphic figure with large eyes and undefined body. Both glyphs are eroded and indistinct. The latter carving, as well as three human designs two metres north were uncovered in 1979 by Daniel Leen, a dedicated rock art researcher.

The first humanoid, a pecked, heart-shaped face, is similar to the carved wooden face masks of Northwest coast groups with its open, circular mouth and heavy eyebrows joined to the nose bridge. Other petroglyph examples of the extended nose line can be viewed at Cedar (DgRw41) and Quadra Island.

Near the mask face Leen uncovered two pecked glyphs, an eroded bear-like face and a large-headed, running humanoid. This active figure displays finely carved toes and fingers as well as a pecked necklace on its long neck. The human's solidly pecked body is unique to the Gabriola Weldwood Site. Again, the connected eyebrows and nose are prominent.

During 1977 we found three carvings of close proximity under a moss and lichen layer (Inset Map C). The very faint, but graceful carving of a mythical humanoid has a shamanistic head projection and animal ear. According to Hill the X-ray rib style used in petroglyphs such as this may symbolize the skeletons of dead people.

The second, an undefined figure, which our children with their twentieth-century bias labelled, "Donald Duck," is very eroded. A head with plumes or feathers, three-toed feet and a circular heart are visible.

The third carving resembles a simple image of a grouse, a local species often seen near the Gabriola Weldwood Site. Hill has suggested that depictions of birds may have represented souls of dead people.

On a searing August day, two years after the first discoveries, we almost renewed the initial excitement with another significant find (Inset Map C). Under 10 cm of dirt and dried grass a wolf-like quadruped was unearthed. Only the X-ray style backbone of this fluidly stylized design has eroded. The ears, oval eyes and downturned snout are similar to the features of the faint quadruped in Section B.

A mysterious spear-like projection topped with a circle extends above the quadruped's back. A variation of this spur and circle design is also visible on the "Rain God" or mythical beast carving at Kulleet Bay, Vancouver Island (DgRw37).

Other quadruped carvings at nearby Petroglyph Park, Nanaimo, resemble the Gabriola Weldwood Site design stylistically. In these carvings the uniting of wolf and serpent characteristics exemplifies the native belief that many animals had dual personalities. The animal's snake-like tail, long sharp muzzle and protruding tongue are reminiscent of totem pole depictions of wolves.

The interpretation of petroglyphs through native myths is an important method of understanding rock art. Jenness describes a Coast Salish legend in which the "mighty trickster and transformer," Khaals, turned a man and his family into the first wolves and gave them the power to grant hunting skill to future generations of man. The killer-whale and wolf were revered for their hunting proficiency and shamans or hunters in training may have carved their images to gain mastery of these powers and to acquire the spirit as a guardian and protector.

South of the mythical animal a second quadruped was uncovered in 1979 by Leen. This deeply abraded carving has a dog-like tail and ears yet the hind leg ends in a bird's talon. Near the small glyph Leen also discovered a strange, deeply carved design that resembles a supernatural head. Three-fingered hands appear to be holding a partial six-rayed sun in this smoothed line petroglyph.

Below the wolf-like quadruped's tail we uncovered a small, deeply abraded head. Evidence of a three-fingered hand exists but most detail below the head has fractured off. The whimsical face has large animal ears and shamanistic rays emerge from the head like antlers, both characteristic features of Northwest coast petroglyphs. Keithahn noted that supernatural people were often depicted with prominent, animal ears in Indian art.

The close proximity and similar carving style of the wolf-like creature and human head may represent the carver's

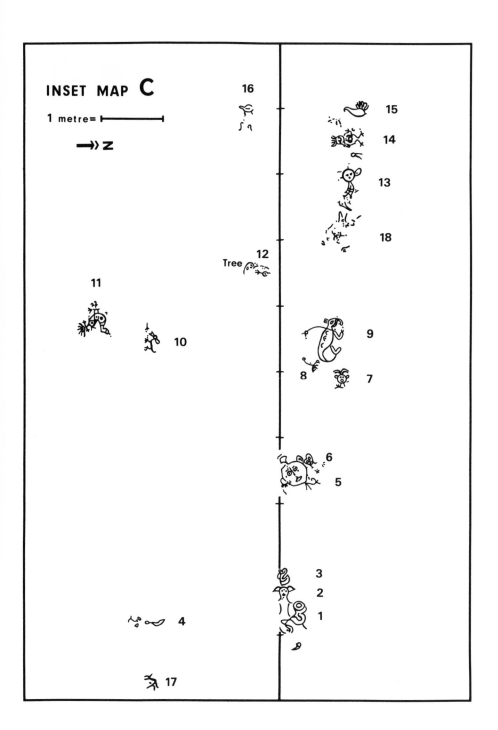

INSET MAP C

1 metre=⊢━━━━━┥

→》z

16
Tree 12
11
10
15
14
13
18
9
8 7
6
5
3
2
1
4
17

47

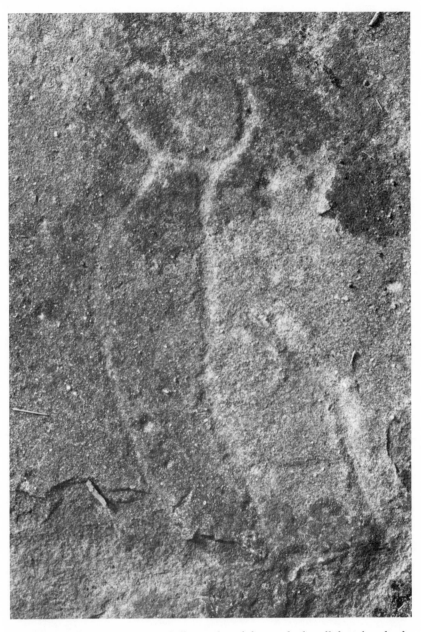

This 25 cm by 60 cm, gracefully outlined figure lacks all facial or body detail and was found under a rotting log.

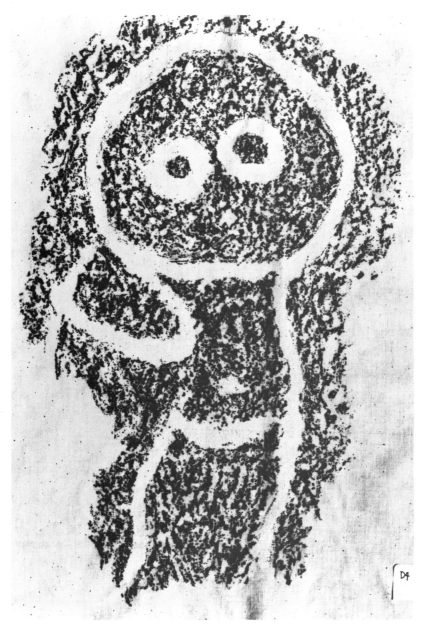

This 30 cm by 65 cm anthropomorph is eroded and indistinct.

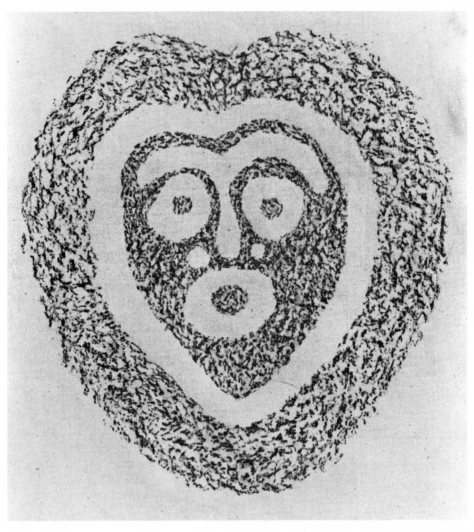

This pecked, heart-shaped face is similar to the carved wooden face masks of the Northwest coast.

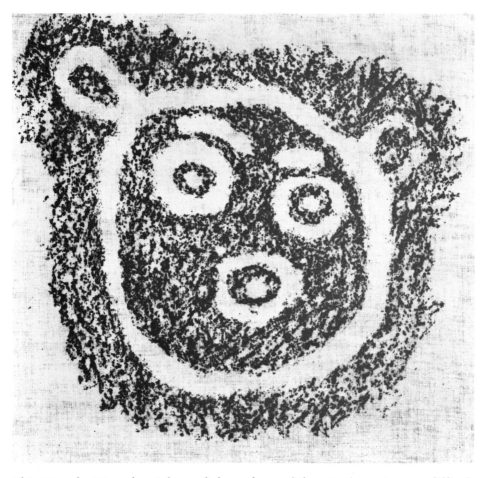

This 25 cm by 28 cm face is located above the mask face. Both carvings are difficult to distinguish.

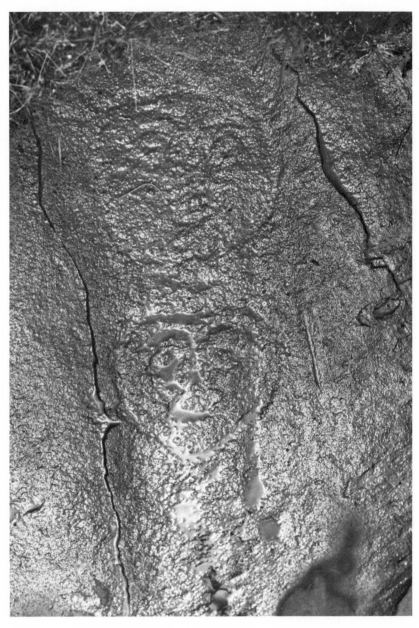

Mask face (below) and bear-like face (above).

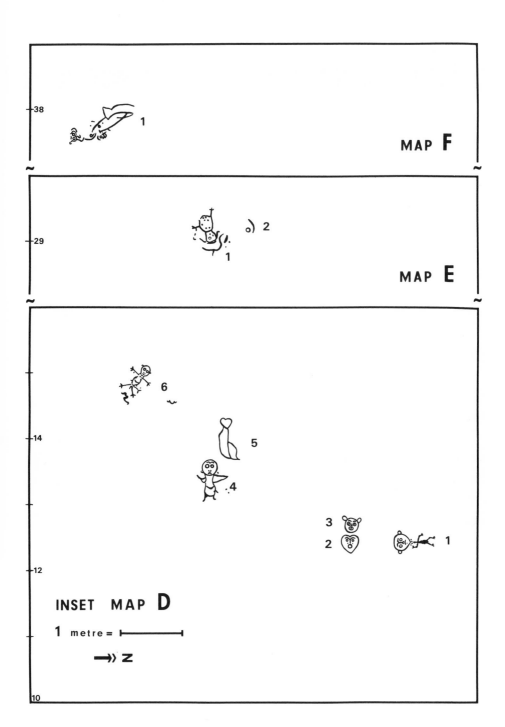

MAP **F**

MAP **E**

INSET MAP **D**

1 metre =

➡》 Z

53

This 35 cm by 50 cm humanoid displays finely carved toes and fingers as well as a necklace.

10-15 cm of earth covered this petroglyph.

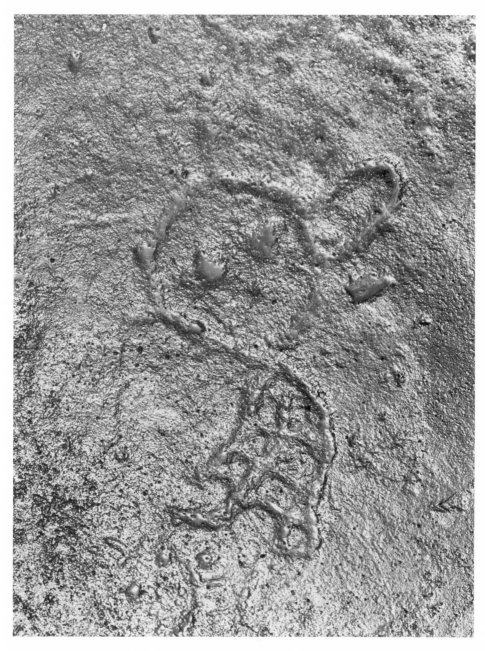

This mythical humanoid, 40 cm by 55 cm, has a shamanistic head projection and one animal ear.

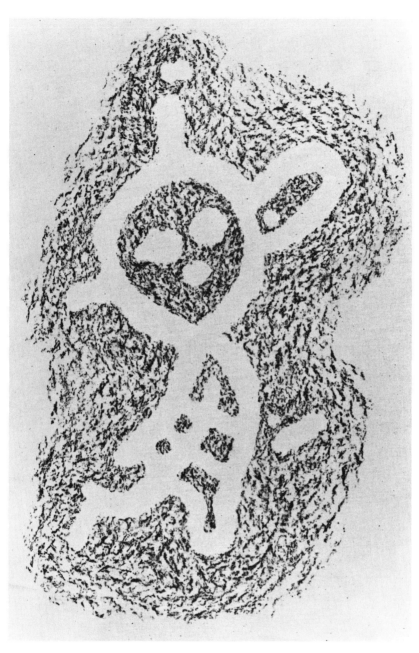

The X-ray rib style may symbolize the skeletons of dead people.

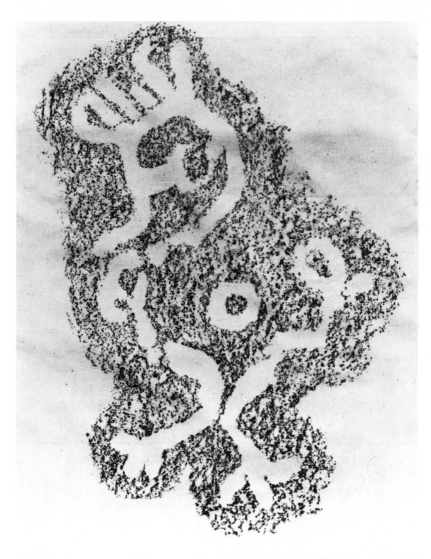

With their twentieth century bias our children labelled this bird-like carving, "Donald Duck."

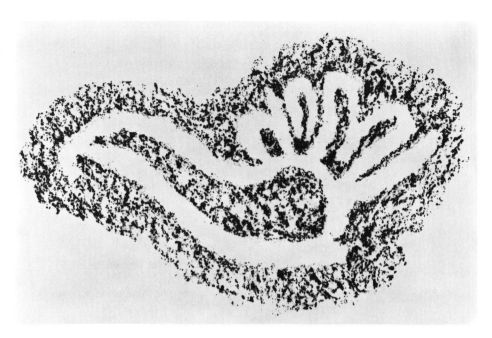

The carving resembles a simple image of a grouse.

Under 10 cm of dirt, a wolf-like quadruped, 40 cm by 60 cm, was unearthed.

The wolf was revered for its hunting proficiency and was believed to live in human societies like the salmon.

A deeply abraded, 20 cm by 30 cm, quadruped.

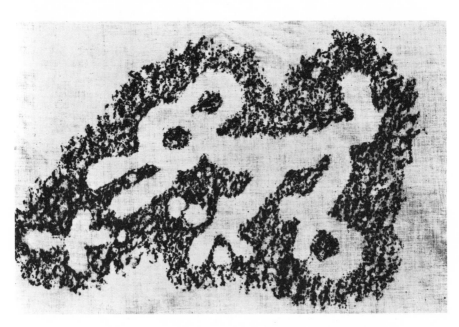

A rubbing of the previous quadruped rock carving.

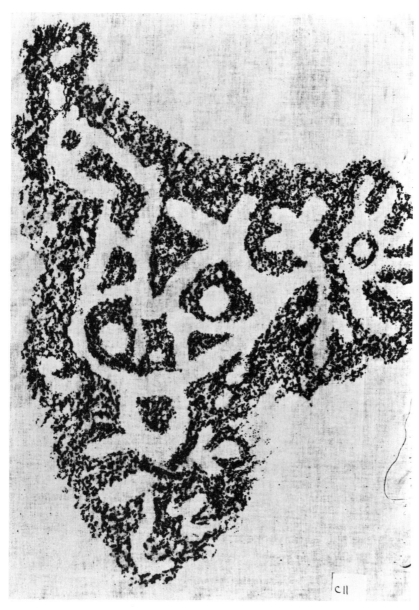

This strange design resembles a supernatural head. Three-fingered hands appear to be holding a partial rayed sun.

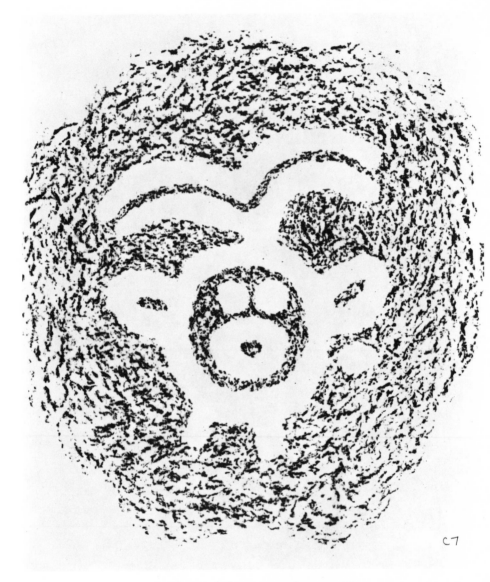

C7

Rubbing of shamanistic humanoid.

A deeply incised head, 25 cm by 25 cm, with shamanistic rays was found near the mythical quadruped.

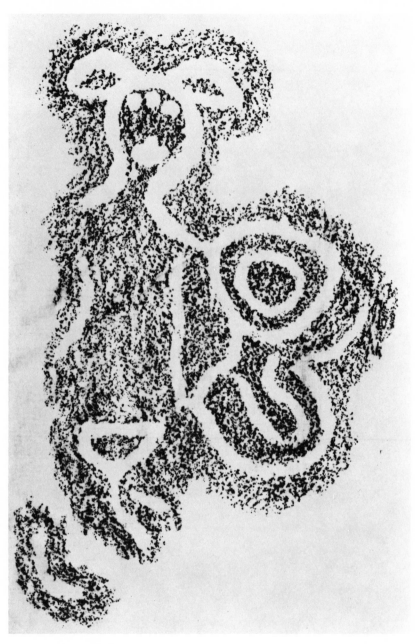

Rubbing of head and meandering lines.

Meandering curves and concentric circles surround a 26 cm by 30 cm mythical head with three eyes and animal ears.

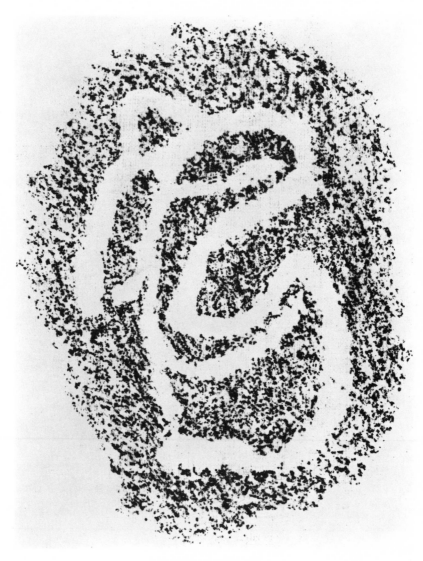

Rubbing of snake-like curves.

This 60 cm by 60 cm eroded carving depicts a head with crest. Near the right ear a small face can barely be distinguished.

A huge mythical creature was uncovered in 1980.

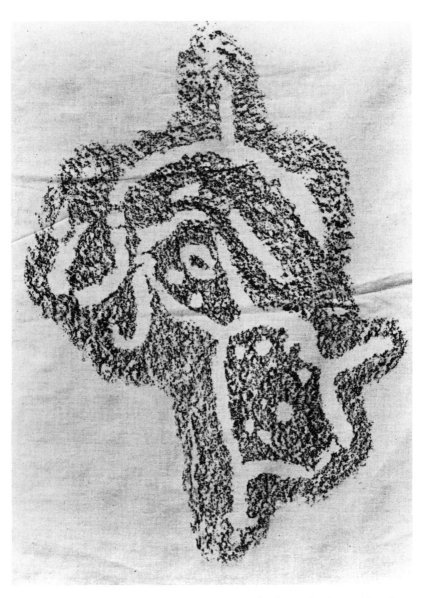

This eroded carving might represent a body with plumed head.

This 12 cm by 22 cm eye and brow illustrates the pecked line technique of carving. The glyph has a depth of 4 mm.

attempt to place himself within the aura of the animal's powerful spirit. A similar juxtaposition, salmon with human, can be seen in Section B.

Another strange, mythical head with pointed ears and three eyes was recorded east of the antlered head. The deeply carved face has a mouth, possibly a labret, and partial body outlines.

Concentric circles, similar to those seen at Petroglyph Park are barely visible to the right of the head. Meandering snake-like curves were pecked above the three-eyed head and all three designs were buried under 12-15 cm of dirt and grass. In 1888 G. T. Emmons recorded a large petroglyph panel on Baranof Island, Alaska, which consisted of many spirals and concentric circles, a typical feature of the area. According to his Tlingit informant, the spiral represented "where the sun comes from" and the concentric circles, the earth. It is probable the entire cluster of carvings recounted the myth of creation.

East of the antlered head and wolf-like quadruped Leen uncovered a large pecked face with circular head crest in 1979. The eroded carving is extremely difficult to see. Near the right ear a small, pecked face can barely be distinguished.

In the summer of 1980 some unknown visitors to the Site uncovered a huge mythical sea creature west of the angular style humanoid. Unfortunately, surface spalling or exfoliation has destroyed the entire tail section of the glyph and no evidence of the missing carved layers could be found.

The deeply abraded creature displays vertical X-ray rib markings similar to those on the large fish in Section A. The strange, bulbous head has detailed markings and the entire glyph is 119 cm by 69 cm. It is possible the carving was inspired by a seal or sea lion with the short curved line on the torso representing a flipper.

West of the large sea creature a possible body and plumed head was discovered (Inset Map E).

A thin layer of lichen partially covered the pecked glyph. Two eyes are discernible but the carving is eroded and indistinct.

Near this undetermined carving a single eye and brow was found under 5 cm of moss. This well preserved glyph is carved to a depth of 4 mm.

To date the westernmost petroglyph recorded at the Site is a faintly pecked fish design surrounded by various circles (possibly eyes) and curves (Inset Map F).

By 1980 over fifty separate petroglyphs were recorded at the Site. Eight unique faces and six fascinating humanoids make up the anthropomorphic images while two bird-like creatures, seven fish, three quadrupeds, two mythical sea creatures and one crab-like carving comprise the zoomorphic representations. Geometric, symbolic or abstract designs such as the foot, eyes, rayed circles, concentric circles, S shapes, ovoids, curves and lines comprise the third catagory of petroglyph types.

It is interesting to note that most anthropomorphic figures at the Site are oriented in a western direction while most sea creatures face eastward.

Typical stylistic features of the carvings are humans with shamanistic head crests or rays, three fingers or toes, animal ears and emphasized eye and head size. The motifs of circle faces, solitary eyes, curvilinear lines and X-ray ribs seen at the Site form a style tradition called *Basic Coast Conventionalized* by anthropologist Doris Lundy.

The most common eye treatment is a single circle, single dot or combination of these while only two quadrupeds and one humanoid head have oval shaped eyes.

Only one carving, a running humanoid in Section D, has a solidly pecked body—all others exhibit outlined features.

Carvings at the Site are equally divided between the pecked line style and smoothed line style. Most pecked carvings have a shallow line depth (½-2 mm) while most abraded line carvings have a depth of 3-5 mm. It seems probable that many pecked carvings were executed at a later time and not initially carved to the depth of the smoothed line carvings.

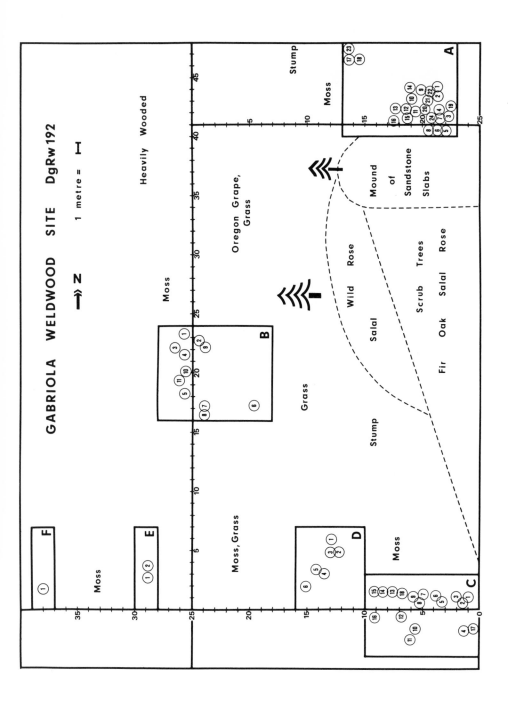

GABRIOLA WELDWOOD SITE DgRw192

N

1 metre = I

# TYPOLOGY OF GABRIOLA ISLAND GLYPHS *
# WELDWOOD SITE

## ANTHROPOMORPHIC

### Full Figures

A14

B5

D6

C13

D1

D4

### Heads

C7

C2

D2

C5
C6

D3

B6

B9

## ZOOMORPHIC

### Sea Creatures

A11

A7

A2

B3

B2

B4

A18

A21

F1

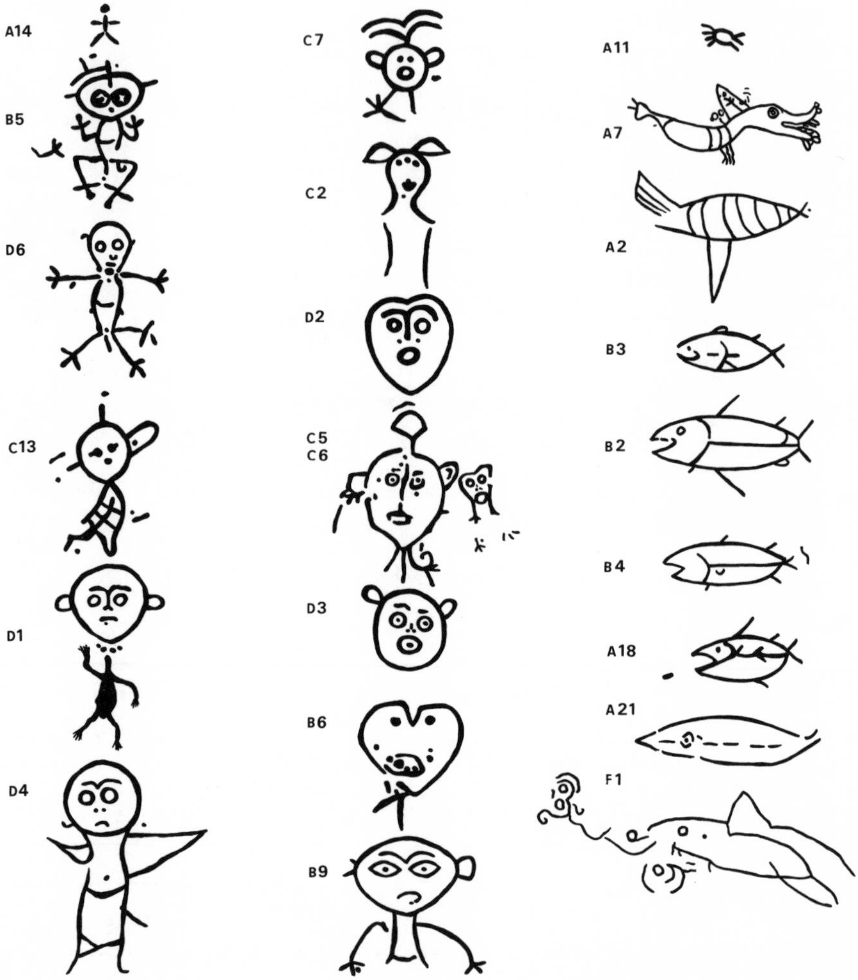

* Drawings not to scale

## Quadrupeds

B7

C9

C10

## Bird-Like

A10

C15

## GEOMETRIC or SYMBOLIC

### Feet

A12

### Eyes

A17

E2

A8

## Suns

A19

A5

B1

## Circles, Lines, Curves, Ovoids

C1

C4

C3

C12

A6

C8

A16

A15

C16

A9

A23

A4

A3

A13

A1

C17

## UNDETERMINED

E1

D5

C14

C11

A20

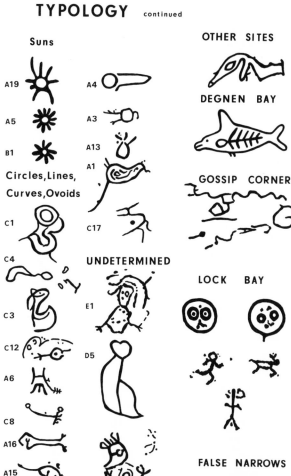

## OTHER SITES

## DEGNEN BAY

## GOSSIP CORNER

## LOCK BAY

## FALSE NARROWS

77

# OTHER GABRIOLA ISLAND PETROGLYPH SITES

Gabriola Island's most familiar petroglyph, interpreted as a "killer-whale" by local residents, is located in Degnen Bay (DgRw2). The carving points seaward and is situated near the end of the Bay where a small stream flows during the winter months. The glyph was carved five metres below high tide line on a sloping slab of sandstone bedrock.

Mr. and Mrs. Harold Cliffe, our parents, own the property below which the killer-whale is carved.

The enjoyment the family derived from observing this solitary, tide washed carving through all seasons for over a decade eventually inspired us to photograph and record all the Island petroglyphs.

The killer-whale was first documented on August 18, 1874, by provincial surveyor John J. Landale, who recorded, "...to tail of Indian carving of seal on rock..." as a section line marking point.

In the early 1900's a wharf beside the petroglyph provided moorage for the Degnens' sloop and steamboats in their produce hauling business. The late Eleanor Holland, a life long resident of Degnen Bay, said her uncle, Frank Degnen, deepened the lines of the killer-whale because he feared the carving had become too faint to identify.

In the 1940's local companies dumped logs at this Site. In spite of this the glyph remains in excellent condition today. Over the past 16 years the Cliffes have noticed no appreciable erosion despite the washing of tides twice daily.

In my opinion few petroglyphs match the simple artistry of this design. Like the Jack Point fish carvings, the X-ray style is distinct. The glyph's large dorsal fin and round eye are features of the killer-whale in Kwakiutl and Haida art according to Boas.

However, the porpoise nose of the carving is an atypical characteristic.

Could designs such as this have been carved to greet and honour the Salmon People at each high tide as the author, Keithahn suggests?

Above the ridge at Gossip Corner a faint carving, 40 cm by 75 cm, was discovered in 1977 by Mabel Cliffe. The shallow, pecked line style is evident but the map-like design is undistinguishable.

On private land at the southern end of the Island (DgRw30), we recorded an exposed bedrock carving of a snake or serpent. The pecked glyph is eroded and faint but an oval eye is distinct. Nearby is a wide, cylindrical hole in the otherwise flat bedrock. This naturally formed basin is deep and cool and may have been ritually used in association with the petroglyph. A similar bowl shaped hole was uncovered at the Gabriola Weldwood Site in 1979. The front lip of this deep basin seems to have been worked and smoothed perhaps from the sharpening of hammerstones.

In 1974 a curious rock containing eroded glyphs was discovered during the road construction of a new hillside subdivision. The solitary sandstone boulder lies in a ditch above False Narrows. The rock probably fractured off the hillside above, where it commanded an impressive ocean vista.

In the fall the central portion of the carving was destroyed. A deeply abraded heart with radiating ribs, an eye and possible mouth or nose remain. Concentric circles and V-shaped lines are also evident.

Four interesting petroglyphs, known to local residents, can be viewed in Lock Bay (DhRw13) on the northern coast of Gabriola Island. The first two carvings are situated along a beautiful, cedar lined, sandy beach.

A pair of forlorn faces, dwarfed by huge surrounding driftwood logs, are carved into the west side of a large sandstone boulder. Situated above high tide line at the forest's edge, the rock is almost concealed by driftwood.

The barely visible, eroded faces do not point seaward which suggests that the rock has possibly shifted. Both faces have large, lonely eyes and labret-like mouths. Circle faces such as these were often associated with salmon streams and fishing

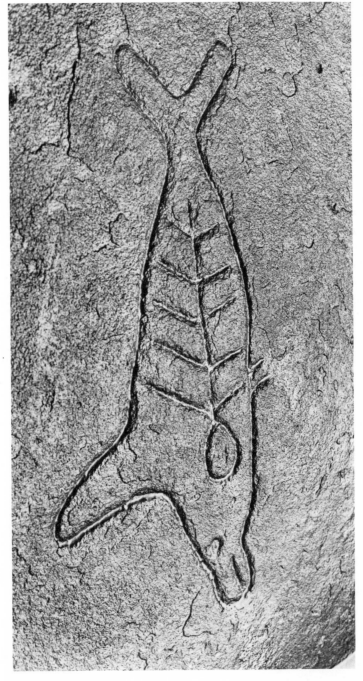

Located near a stream mouth in Degnen Bay, this 65 cm by 120 cm "killer-whale" is covered twice daily by tides.

Rubbing of killer-whale.

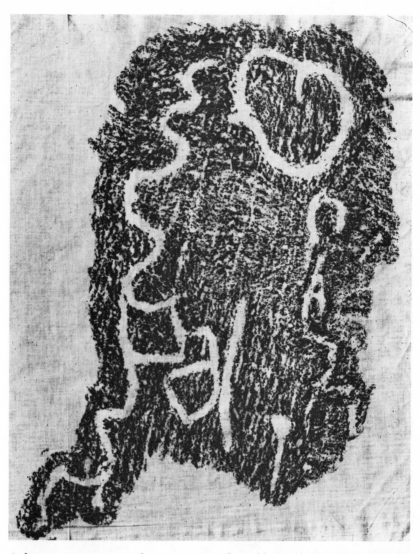

A faint carving, 40 cm by 75 cm, was found by Mabel Cliffe at Gossip Corner.

This pecked serpent or snake is eroded and faint.

A bowl shaped hole at the Gabriola Weldwood Site.

Rubbing of the petroglyph boulder near False Narrows.

The 2½ m by 1 m rock probably fractured off the hillside above thus destroying part of the carved designs.

Geometric and abstract shapes are visible as well as ribs, heart and eye.

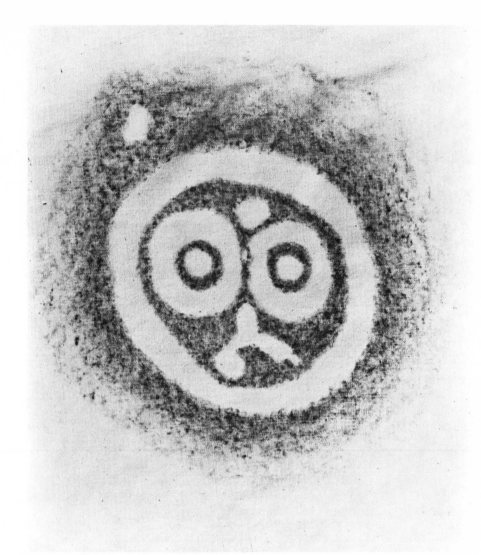

A pair of small faces, each about 20 cm by 20 cm were carved into the west side of a sandstone boulder in Lock Bay.

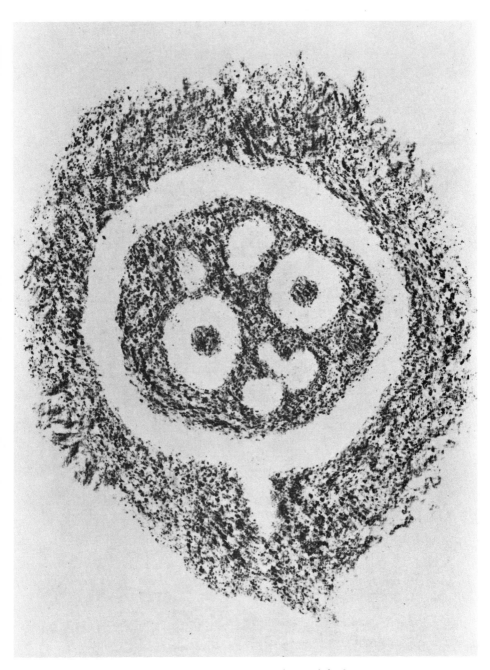

Both faces have labret-like mouths and forlorn eyes.

A natural bowl-shaped depression on top of the boulder may have been used to grind ocher for ceremonials.

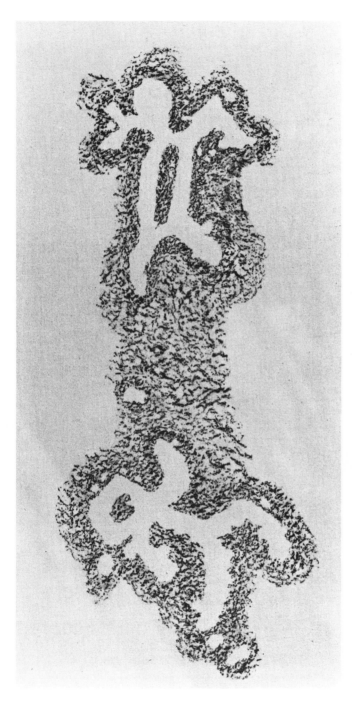

Carvings depicting hunting scenes are stylistically atypical in Northwest coast petroglyph designs. This deeply pecked glyph is located in Lock Bay, Gabriola Island.

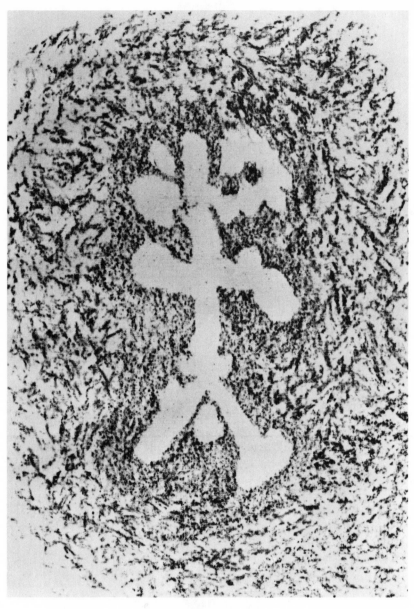

This small, eroded stick figure is located in Lock Bay.

places. A natural bowl shaped depression on top of the rock is similar to those seen at the Weldwood Site as well as DgRw30. It is conceivable that the existence of the bowl shape inspired the initial carving of petroglyphs.

Near the faces an interesting and somewhat controversial carving of a man chasing a deer is deeply pecked on a sloping sandstone rock which is imbedded in sand at high tide line.

The design is 70 cm by 27 cm and pecked to a depth of 9 mm, three times the depth of most petroglyphs on the Island, suggesting perhaps that a metal tool was used. While the glyph is unlikely to be as old as the faces, a local land owner told Beth Hill it had been on the beach throughout the fifty years of his knowledge.

Carvings depicting hunting scenes are stylistically atypical in Northwest coast petroglyph designs. They are, however, similar to the pictographs of British Columbia's interior, the Kootenay Lake Sites being an example.

In 1978 two Island visitors drew our attention to a small petroglyph they had found in Lock Bay. The eroded stick figure is situated on a large boulder at high tide line. The design resembles a male humanoid with a rayed head-dress.

# THE ENIGMA

Petroglyphs remain one of the least understood cultural legacies of Northwest coast native people. Their purpose can only be surmised; their age cannot be reliably determined except in rare historic examples; and ethnographic information is almost non-existent. Native people told archaeologist, Harlan I. Smith, in 1920 that petroglyphs were created "before animals were transformed into men."

Recorded observations of an Indian carving a petroglyph are rare which deepens the enigma. With the advent of European white man's civilization on the Northwest coast rock carving gradually terminated.

Petroglyphs have been found worldwide: in European caves, on the Hawaiian Islands, in South America, Africa, Australia, Asia, Scandinavia, and throughout North America.

The distribution of petroglyphs in the Northwest generally follows the coastline from northern Alaska southward to the Columbia River area. A consistent rock carving style is evident throughout this coastal region as well as along the lower reaches of the Fraser and Columbia Rivers.

In British Columbia's interior the art of pictographs or painting images on stone with red ocher compounds (hematite) is more prevalent. Here a contrasting style of design and subject matter can be seen although some of the reasons for carving petroglyphs parallel those of rock paintings.

Petroglyphs exist on many of the Gulf Islands. This chain of mild-climated isles is situated between the mainland and Vancouver Island. Rock art sites are also scattered along the western and eastern coastlines of Vancouver Island.

Ancient Indian carvers selected specific, although diverse,

locations for petroglyphs: on an ocean beach; at a stream mouth, waterfall or lake shore; or near a cave, bluff or other odd rock formation such as a bedrock bowl shape. Shoreline glyphs usually face the sea and many are covered daily by rising tides.

Less frequently the sites were isolated, inland areas which may have functioned as spiritual training centres for shamans or priests. The Coast Salish belief in the eternal spirit power of rocks to move, to contain curses and to transform creatures prevented uninitiated members of the community from visiting these shrines. The large number of petroglyphs seen at these sacred sites is an indication of the area's importance for it was believed that spirit power increased with each carving. It is our theory that the inland Gabriola Weldwood Site which conveys an aura of mystery and seclusion may have been chosen by shamans as such a sacred centre.

The type of rock chosen for carvings on the Northwest coast was usually sandstone, a soft, coarse-grained sedimentary rock, predominent on the Gulf Islands. On Quadra Island, near Campbell River, petroglyphs were cut into the hard granite boulders which are abundant on its beaches. Less often, basalt rocks were used as a medium.

Shamans pecked their designs into the sandstone with various sizes of sharpened hammerstones. Some carvings were deliberately abandoned at this stage, the lines of the image being a series of small holes. There are many examples of this carving technique at the Gabriola Weldwood Site. In other glyphs like the serpent the pecked line was smoothed into a deep, 2 cm wide groove.

In most cases it is impossible to accurately date petroglyphs. No scientific techniques have, as yet, been devised to calculate the age of the pecked grooves in rocks.

A small percentage of Northwest coast carvings have been dated to the historic period. In *Indian Petroglyphs of the Pacific Northwest*, Hill discusses the carvings of sailing ships and the paddle-wheel steamship, *Beaver*, observed on the west coast of Vancouver Island around 1836. The awed and alarmed Nootkan Indians recorded these events in stone near Clo-oose.

At Fort Rupert, Vancouver Island, a face was ritually carved during a Winter Ceremonial in the same period. This was witnessed by Hudson's Bay Company officials and documented by Boas.

In 1975, researcher Ann McMurdo reported that a midden excavation on Protection Island (DhRx5) unearthed a petroglyph which was carved around 1600 A.D. The undisturbed stratified layers of midden deposits above the carving allowed the first accurate Carbon 14 petroglyph dating in British Columbia to be established.

In the past decade investigation has been made into many petroglyph dating theories such as the degree of erosion, the depth of soil coverings, stylistic relationships and subject matter comparisons. Some theories such as the study of lichen growth over carvings or paintings and the degree of patination, changes in the rock's natural surface colour, have not yet produced conclusive results.

While at first observation it might seem that very faint carvings are the most ancient, the differences of line depth from one glyph to another could also be the result of dissimilar initial carving depths or dissimilar weathering by frost action, soil coverage, drainage and exposure to tides.

Although the serpent and mythical bird glyphs at the Gabriola Weldwood Site are deeply carved showing very little erosion, other nearby petroglyphs are so faint their outlines can only be detected in the fading, angular light of dusk. It seems probable that many faint glyphs were never initially carved as deeply as others and that the serpent and mythical bird may be older glyphs because of their central placement on the rock surface.

It is tempting to gauge a carving's age from the amount of earth covering it. Hill discusses a Site discovered in 1969 near the Nanaimo River (DgRx8) with a soil depth of about 30 cm which was given a hypothetical age of up to 1000 years by provincial observers.

A soil covering of up to 20 cm was the maximum depth we recorded at the Gabriola Weldwood Site. In contrast, some carvings were hidden by only a layer of paper thin moss. Since logging took place on and around this Site the natural progression of soil accumulation has been disturbed, therefore dating by soil depths would probably be difficult.

As more and more carving sites are accurately reported and

recorded, research into subject matter comparisons and style relationships of Northwest coast petroglyphs may prove to be the most promising method of answering the dating mystery. Currently these style comparisons and distributions suggest a probable date of 2000-3000 B.C. for our oldest petroglyph tradition. According to Hill some glyphs "may be as old as the history of men on this coast" but an unawareness of their exact age need not detract from our appreciation of their artistry and elegance.

Vandalism at the Gabriola Weldwood Site.

One of the authors producing a rubbing of the mythical creature. (KAREN CLIFFE)

# PROTECTION

In recent years there has been an awakening of public interest in Northwest coast rock art. Many visitors to accessible petroglyph sites have been taking rubbings of the carvings. It is important to contact the Heritage Conservation Branch in Victoria and obtain a written permit to take rubbings before visiting a site. Remember to use only crayons or cobbler's wax and never paints of any kind. At the site be extremely careful not to walk on any carvings. Petroglyphs that have been carved into sandstone bedrock are susceptible to sheeting and cracking. Never outline the image with chalk as a means of seeing the design more clearly. Respect other visitors' wish to view the petroglyphs naturally without modern man's additions. Also, a chalk outlined glyph invites serious damage by less responsible people using paint or other permanent markers.

The 1977 British Columbia Heritage Conservation Act protects any petroglyph site whether on private or Crown land. It states, "no person shall knowingly destroy or deface an Indian painting or carving on rock." The penalty upon conviction is two thousand dollars or imprisonment for a term not exceeding six months or both. The Act is a necessary deterrent against vandals and relic hunters.

California petroglyphs have not been well protected and as a result desert glyphs in the Colorado River Valley carved by fourteenth- or fifteenth-century Yuman Indians have been dynamited and broken away by souvenir hunters.

Another unfortunate case involved the San Jacinto Museum which, in 1978, ordered the removal by jackhammering of a rare maze design petroglyph boulder from the Lakeview Mountains area. The town wished to place the carved section of the stone in front of its new museum. Unfortunately, to the dismay of local archaeologists and the Soboba Band of Mission Indians, the jackhammering accidentally fractured the rock to the very edge of the carved design. Some groups now wish to return the petroglyph fragment to its original boulder while others fear theft or vandalism.

In British Columbia the Cape Mudge Indian Band of Quadra Island have barged most movable petroglyph boulders from their original beach site to a park in Yaculta Village and will not allow rubbings to be made. Although it is unfortunate the glyphs cannot be viewed in their ancient setting they have now been protected from tide erosion and souvenir hunters.

Since our discovery of the Gabriola Weldwood Site in 1976 numerous disturbing incidents of thoughtless vandalism have taken place. In the summer of 1980 several children scratched names and pictures over two eroded petroglyphs at the Site. It will likely be two or three years before these defacing markings gradually disappear with natural weathering. In 1979 individuals in a four-wheel-drive vehicle drove over the largest panel of petroglyphs in Section A while chopping and collecting firewood illegally. Large boulders now block the entranceway and protect the carvings from being crushed.

On several occasions we have arrived at the Site to find crayon and paint marks in the glyphs' carved lines. Most damage has been caused by people who do not realize the importance of our Northwest coast rock art heritage.

Two philosophies regarding petroglyph sites exist—full public disclosure of site locations versus total denial to the general community. While not completely comfortable with either extreme, we believe that by educating the public, particularly our school children, we can conserve as well as enjoy this priceless part of our native Indian legacy.

# PREHISTORIC PURPOSES OF PETROGLYPHS

Part of the fascination of petroglyphs lies in the mystery of their prehistoric meanings. Several theories are applicable to Northwest coast glyphs.

Individual carvings may have been made to record regional legends and myths such as the Salmon People story on Nanaimo's Jack Point boulder. Keithahn wrote, "Myths and legends that were later used to embellish totem poles were graven much earlier on beach boulders."

Secondly, because carvings are often situated near stream mouths, they may have been engraved to entice spawning schools of salmon. Keithahn pointed out that shoreline petroglyphs almost always face the sea because "they were meant to be seen or read from the water" by the Salmon People. He was informed by Haida Indians in 1939 that some glyphs were carved to evoke rainfall which consequently would expand rivers and stimulate salmon to enter and spawn.

Thirdly, Boas recounts that some petroglyphs were a record of significant events such as a slave killing which took place at Fort Rupert during the Hamatsa or Cannibal Dancer Initiation.

It is probable that some historic period carvings were executed as doodlings or as some researchers have called them, "ancient graffiti." However, it is our opinion that although a few carvings may have served this purpose, the majority of petroglyphs fulfilled important functions.

Probably the most significant purpose petroglyphs achieved was in association with an individual's pursuit of spiritual power and guardian spirits. The ritualist or shaman training site was an isolated, secret area. The Kulleet Bay pool on Vancouver Island (DgRw36), and the Gabriola Weldwood Site suggest such mystical centres where shamans and solitary individuals endured a self-inflicted ordeal of physical torture, praying, fasting, retching and cleansing in an effort to experience hallucinatory visions. Perhaps the young carver hoped to acquire the strength of the spirit conjured in his trance by incising it on stone.

Author Douglas Leechman describes the spirit quest as a possible function of pictographs as well as petroglyphs. The adolescent may have recorded his mystical visions on stone to exorcise the power of frightening monsters or to retain the forces of guardian spirits.

When the shaman returned to his community he functioned, in Keithahn's words, "as a dedicated individual . . . convinced of his supernatural powers and relied upon by his people. He attended the sick, ferreted out witches, advised the chief and accompanied war parties."

Modern society's comprehension of the enigmatical petroglyph may always be clouded with ambiguity because of the personal nature of these rituals. In 1963 Keithahn wrote of the riddle, "Perhaps because their true meaning and import is so elusive, students have in general belittled them. Most scholars have done little more than noted their existence and dismissed them as the doodlings of primitive man." The last ten years has seen an explosion of interest and scientific research into North American rock art. As more and more sites are accurately recorded and this data is shared by anthropologists, important correlations and analyses into style traditions and age seriation can be made.

The Canadian Rock Art Research Associates, founded in 1969 by the late Selwyn Dewdney and other scholars, has stimulated and supported much research through its Newsletter and national conferences. The aims of C.R.A.R.A. are "to protect and preserve rock art sites in Canada, to promote Canadian rock art research and to inform the Canadian public of its aboriginal art heritage." Membership in the C.R.A.R.A. organization can be obtained by writing:

C.R.A.R.A., Secretary-Treasurer
Department of Anthropology and Archaeology
University of Saskatchewan
Saskatoon, Saskatchewan, Canada
S7N 0W0

While the precise meaning and exact age of most petroglyphs can only be surmised by today's experts, the elegance of design and mysterious atmosphere of isolated sites compel our admiration and respect.

Petroglyphs require the public's awareness and preservation. Future generations deserve the rich rock art legacy of our native forefathers. As Wilson Duff wrote in *Images: Stone: B.C.*, "Stone's lastingness makes it a proper medium for man's eternal truths."

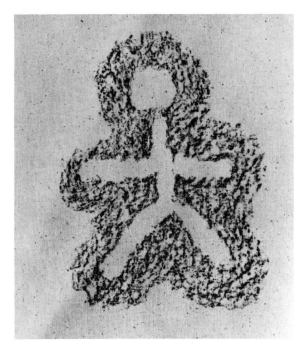

Anthropomorphic glyph—rubbing.

# APPENDIX

The mythical bird in December—note the ice covering the lower half of the carving.

# NUMERICAL DATA

| WELDWOOD SITE | Map Location | Compass Orientation | Dimensions cm | Line Depth mm | Line Width cm | Carving Style | | Preservation | | |
|---|---|---|---|---|---|---|---|---|---|---|
| | | | | | | Pecked Holes | Abraded and Smoothed | Excellent | Fairly Visible | Eroded and Indistinct |
| **Anthropomorphic** | | | | | | | | | | |
| **Full Figures** | | | | | | | | | | |
| Stick figure | A 14 | E | 17 x 22 | 2 | 1 | x | | | x | |
| Male humanoid | B 5 | W | 35 x 55 | 3 | 1½ | | x | | x | |
| Humanoid | D 6 | NW | 40 x 50 | 2 | 1 | x | | | x | |
| Mythical humanoid | C 13 | W | 40 x 55 | 2 | 1 | | x | | | x |
| Humanoid | D 1 | S | 35 x 50 | 3 | 1 | x | | | x | |
| Humanoid | D 4 | W | 30 x 65 | 2 | 1 | x | | | | x |
| **Heads** | | | | | | | | | | |
| Antlered head | C 7 | W | 25 x 25 | 5 | 1½ | | x | x | | |
| Three-eyed head | C 2 | W | 26 x 30 | 4 | 1 | | x | x | | |
| Mask face | D 2 | W | 28 x 30 | 2 | 1 | x | | | x | |
| Large head with small face | C 5 C 6 | SW | 60 x 60 | 2 | 1 | x | | | | x |
| Bear-like face | D 3 | W | 25 x 28 | 1 | 1 | x | | | | x |
| Face with teeth | B 6 | E | 32 x 40 | 4 | 1 | | x | x | | |
| Head and arms | B 9 | S | 38 x 38 | ½ | 1 | x | | | | x |
| **Zoomorphic** | | | | | | | | | | |
| **Sea Creatures** | | | | | | | | | | |
| Crab | A 11 | - | 9 x 17 | 2 | 1 | x | | | x | |
| Serpent | A 7 | E | 100 x 255 | 5 | 2 | | x | x | | |
| Ribbed fish | A 2 | E | 130 x 200 | 4 | 1 | | x | x | | |
| Salmon | B 3 | E | 17 x 40 | ½ | 1 | x | | | | x |
| Salmon | B 2 | E | 35 x 70 | ½ | 1 | x | | | | x |
| Salmon | B 4 | E | 22 x 52 | ½ | 1 | x | | | | x |
| Fish, curves | F 1 | SE | 20 x 140 | 1 | 1 | x | | | | x |
| Fish shape | A 21 | E | 18 x 25 | ½ | 1 | x | | | | x |
| Salmon | A 18 | N | 15 x 30 | 2 | 1 | x | | | | x |
| Seal-like | D 7 | NW | 69 x 119 | 5 | 1½ | | x | x | | |
| **Quadrupeds** | | | | | | | | | | |
| Wolf-like quad. | C 9 | NW | 40 x 60 | 4 | 1½ | | x | x | | |
| Small quadruped | C 10 | W | 20 x 30 | 4 | 1½ | | x | x | | |
| Mythical creature | B 7 | E | 40 x 55 | 2 | 1 | x | | | | x |
| **Bird-Like** | | | | | | | | | | |
| Mythical bird | A 10 | NW | 72 x 114 | 5 | 2 | | x | x | | |
| Grouse-like bird | C 15 | S | 20 x 30 | 3 | 1 | x | | | x | |

| Geometric, Abstract or Symbolic Figures | Map Location | Compass Orientation | Line Depth mm | Dimensions cm | Line Width cm | Carving Style Pecked Holes | Abraded and Smoothed | Excellent | Fairly Visible | Eroded and Indistinct |
|---|---|---|---|---|---|---|---|---|---|---|
| **Feet** | | | | | | | | | | |
| Foot | A12 | SE | 10 x 22 | 1 | 1 | x | | | | x |
| **Eyes** | | | | | | | | | | |
| Eyes, brow, nose | A17 | SW | 14 x 22 | 3 | 1 | x | | x | | |
| Eye, brow | E 2 | N | 12 x 22 | 4 | 1 | x | | x | | |
| Eyes, nose line | A 8 | NE | 10 x 13 | 1 | 1 | | x | | | x |
| **Suns** | | | | | | | | | | |
| 11 rayed sun | A 5 | - | 14 x 14 | 2 | 1 | | x | | | x |
| 8 rayed sun | B 1 | - | 12 x 12 | ½ | 1 | x | | | | x |
| 8 rayed sun | A19 | - | 25 x 25 | 3 | 1 | x | | | | x |
| **Circles, Ovoids, Curves or Lines** | | | | | | | | | | |
| Curves, circle | A23 | - | 10 x 32 | ½ | 1 | x | | | | x |
| Circles, curves | C 1 | - | 20 x 35 | 1 | 1 | | x | | | x |
| Curves | C 4 | - | 12 x 44 | 4 | 1 | | x | x | | |
| Curves | C 3 | - | 20 x 30 | 2 | 1 | x | | | | x |
| Circles, curves | C12 | - | 60 x 25 | 3 | 1 | x | | | x | |
| Lines, curves | A 6 | - | 13 x 15 | 4 | 1½ | | x | x | | |
| Circles, lines | C 8 | - | 15 x 35 | 2 | 1 | x | | | | x |
| Curves | A16 | - | 12 x 30 | 2 | 1 | x | | | | x |
| Curves | A15 | - | 15 x 30 | 3 | 1½ | x | | | x | |
| Curves | C16 | - | 15 x 20 | 2 | 1 | x | | | | x |
| V shape | A 9 | - | 15 x 18 | 5 | 1 | | x | x | | |
| Curves, lines | A 3 | - | 15 x 35 | 3 | 1 | x | | | | x |
| Ovoid, lines | A13 | - | 14 x 16 | 1 | 1 | x | | | | x |
| Ovoid, eye | A 1 | W | 28 x 45 | 5 | 1 | | x | x | | |
| Curves | A22 | - | 25 x 30 | ½ | 1 | x | | | | x |
| Circles, line | A24 | - | 17 x 20 | ½ | 1 | x | | | | x |
| Lines, dots | B 8 | - | 16 x 60 | ½ | 1 | x | | | | x |
| Curves | C17 | - | 25 x 25 | ½ | 1 | | x | | x | |
| Curves, lines | C18 | - | 45 x 45 | ½ | 1 | x | | | | x |
| Forked curves | B10 | - | 30 x 30 | ½ | 1 | | x | | | x |
| Circle | B11 | - | 5 x 5 | 3 | 1 | | x | x | | |
| Circle, lines | A 4 | - | 10 x 23 | 3 | 1 | x | | | | x |
| **Undetermined** | | | | | | | | | | |
| Head, body? | E 1 | - | 40 x 50 | 1 | 1 | x | | | | x |
| Head, body? | D 5 | W | 25 x 60 | 2 | 1½ | | x | | | x |
| Bird-like? | C14 | S | 32 x 52 | 2 | 1 | | x | | | x |
| Head? | C11 | - | 40 x 50 | 4 | 1½ | | x | x | | |
| Zoomorph head? | A20 | - | 25 x 33 | ½ | 1 | x | | | | x |

| OTHER GABRIOLA SITES | Compass Orientation | Dimensions cm | Line Depth mm | Line Width cm | Carving Style | | Preservation | | |
|---|---|---|---|---|---|---|---|---|---|
| | | | | | Pecked Holes | Abraded and Smoothed | Excellent | Fairly Visible | Eroded and Indistinct |
| Killer-whale | SE | 65 x 120 | 5 | 1½ | | x | x | recarved | |
| Geometric | - | 40 x 75 | 2 | 1 | x | | | | x |
| Face | W | 20 x 20 | 3 | 1½ | | x | | x | |
| Face | W | 22 x 22 | 2 | 1½ | | x | | | x |
| Man and deer | W | 27 x 70 | 9 | 1½ | x | | x | | |
| Stick figure | S | 13 x 27 | 5 | 1½ | | x | | x | |
| Undefined | | 45 x 45 | 4 | 1 | | x | | x | |
| Geometric | | 40 x 40 | 4 | 1 | | x | | x | |
| Serpent | SE | 30 x 60 | 2 | ½ | x | | | | x |

# CHART OF UNEARTHED PETROGLYPHS

## Gabriola Weldwood Site

| Map No. | Glyph | Year Recorded or Uncovered | Type of Covering | Maximum Depth | Average Depth |
|---------|-------|------------|-----------------|---------------|---------------|
| A14 | Stick figure | 1977 | moss / grass | 5 cm | 5 cm |
| B  5 | Male humanoid | 1976 | visible / lichen | - | - |
| D  6 | Humanoid | 1977 | moss / grass | 5 cm | 5 cm |
| C13 | Mythical humanoid | 1977 | moss / lichen | 5 cm | 2 cm |
| D  1 | Humanoid | 1979 | grass / dirt | 15 cm | 5 cm |
| D  4 | Humanoid | 1979 | moss / grass | 5 cm | 2 cm |
| | | | | | |
| C  7 | Antlered head | 1978 | grass / dirt | 10 cm | 10 cm |
| C  2 | Three-eyed head | 1978 | grass / dirt | 15 cm | 12 cm |
| D  2 | Mask face | 1978 | moss / dirt | 5 cm | 5 cm |
| C  5 | Large head with | | | | |
| C  6 | small face | 1979 | grass / dirt | 10 cm | 6 cm |
| D  3 | Bear-like face | 1979 | moss / dirt | 5 cm | 5 cm |
| B  6 | Face with teeth | 1979 | grass / dirt | 10 cm | 8 cm |
| B  9 | Head and arms | 1979 | visible | - | - |
| | | | | | |
| A11 | Crab | 1976 | moss / grass / dirt | 12 cm | 12 cm |
| A  7 | Serpent | 1976 | grass / dirt | 20 cm | 12 cm |
| A  2 | Ribbed fish | 1976 | visible / moss | 5 cm | 2 cm |
| B  3 | Salmon | 1976 | visible / lichen | - | - |
| B  4 | Salmon | 1976 | visible / lichen | - | - |
| B  2 | Salmon | 1976 | visible / lichen | - | - |
| F  1 | Fish, curves | 1979 | moss | 3 cm | 3 cm |
| A21 | Fish shape | 1977 | moss / grass | 12 cm | 5 cm |
| A18 | Salmon | 1977 | moss / grass | 8 cm | 8 cm |
| D  7 | Seal-like | 1980 | moss / grass | 8 cm | 4 cm |
| C  9 | Wolf-like quadruped | 1978 | grass / dirt | 10 cm | 6 cm |
| C10 | Small quadruped | 1979 | moss / grass / dirt | 7 cm | 5 cm |
| B  7 | Mythical creature | 1979 | visible | - | - |
| | | | | | |
| A10 | Mythical bird | 1976 | moss / grass | 12 cm | 6 cm |
| C15 | Grouse-like bird | 1977 | moss / lichen | 3 cm | 3 cm |
| | | | | | |
| A12 | Foot | 1977 | moss / grass | 6 cm | 6 cm |
| A17 | Eyes, brows, nose | 1977 | moss / grass | 8 cm | 8 cm |
| E  2 | Eye, brow | 1977 | moss | 5 cm | 5 cm |
| A  8 | Eyes, nose line | 1976 | grass / dirt | 20 cm | 20 cm |
| | | | | | |
| A  5 | Rayed sun | 1976 | grass / dirt | 20 cm | 20 cm |
| B  1 | Rayed sun | 1976 | visible / lichen | - | - |
| A19 | Rayed sun | 1979 | visible | - | - |

| Map No. | Glyph | Year Recorded or Uncovered | Type of Covering | Maximum Depth | Average Depth |
|---------|-------|---------------------------|------------------|---------------|---------------|
| A 23 | Curves, circle | 1979 | moss / grass | 5 cm | 5 cm |
| C 1 | Circles, curves | 1978 | grass / dirt | 15 cm | 15 cm |
| C 4 | Curves | 1979 | moss | 5 cm | 5 cm |
| C 3 | Curves | 1978 | grass / dirt | 12 cm | 12 cm |
| C 12 | Circles, curves | 1979 | moss | 5 cm | 5 cm |
| A 6 | Lines, curves | 1976 | grass / dirt | 20 cm | 20 cm |
| C 8 | Circles, lines | 1978 | grass / dirt | 6 cm | 6 cm |
| A 16 | Curves | 1977 | grass / dirt | 20 cm | 20 cm |
| A 15 | Curves | 1977 | moss / grass | 6 cm | 6 cm |
| C 16 | Curves | 1979 | moss / grass | 5 cm | 5 cm |
| A 9 | V-shape | 1976 | visible / lichen | - | - |
| A 3 | Curves, lines | 1978 | moss / grass | 6 cm | 6 cm |
| A 13 | Ovoid, lines | 1977 | moss / grass | 5 cm | 5 cm |
| A 1 | Ovoid, eye | 1976 | visible | - | - |
| A 22 | Curves | 1977 | moss / grass | 5 cm | 5 cm |
| A 24 | Circles, line | 1976 | grass / dirt | 12 cm | 12 cm |
| B 8 | Lines, dots | 1979 | visible | - | - |
| C 17 | Curves | 1979 | grass / moss | 5 cm | 5 cm |
| C 18 | Curves, lines | 1979 | visible | - | - |
| B 10 | Forked curves | 1979 | visible | - | - |
| B 11 | Circle | 1976 | visible | - | - |
| A 4 | Circle, lines | 1976 | grass / dirt | 12 cm | 12 cm |
| E 1 | Head, body? | 1977 | visible / lichen | - | - |
| D 5 | Head, body? | 1978 | moss/rotting log | 2 cm | 2 cm |
| C 14 | Bird-like? | 1977 | moss / lichen | 5 cm | 5 cm |
| C 11 | Head? | 1979 | grass / dirt | 6 cm | 5 cm |
| A 20 | Zoomorph head? | 1977 | grass / dirt | 12 cm | 12 cm |

**Gossip Corner**

| | Glyph | Year Recorded or Uncovered | Type of Covering | Maximum Depth | Average Depth |
|---|-------|---------------------------|------------------|---------------|---------------|
| | Geometric, abstract | 1977 | moss / dirt | 3 cm | 2 cm |

# SUGGESTED READING

Anati, Emmanuel   1977
*Methods of Recording and Analysing Rock Engravings.* Brescia, Italy:
Edizioni Del Centro.

Boas, Franz   1927
*Primitive Art.* New York: Dover Publications (1955 edition).

Cox, J. Halley and Stasack, E.   1970
*Hawaiian Petroglyphs.* Honolulu: Bishop Museum Press.

Duff, Wilson   1975
*Images: Stone: B.C.* Saanichton: Hancock House.

Drucker, Philip   1965
*Cultures of the North Pacific Coast.* San Francisco: Chandler Publishing.

Emmons, G. T.   1908
"Petroglyphs in Southeastern Alaska." *American Anthropologist,*
no. 10.

Hill, Beth and Hill, Ray   1974
*Indian Petroglyphs of the Pacific Northwest.* Saanichton: Hancock House.

Hill, Beth   1975
*Guide to Indian Rock Carvings of the Pacific Northwest Coast.* Saanichton:
Hancock House.

Hill, Beth   1976
"The Petroglyph Ships." *Westworld,* November-December.

Holm, Bill   1965
*Northwest Coast Indian Art.* Seattle: University of Washington Press.

Jenness, Diamond   1955
*The Faith of a Coast Salish Indian.* Anthropology in B.C. No. 3.

Keithahn, E. L.   1939
"Secret of the Petroglyphs." *Alaska Sportsman,* March.

Keithahn, E. L.   1963
*Monuments in Cedar*. Seattle: Superior Publishing. Reprinted.

Lawrence, Scott   1976
"Petroglyphs." *Raincoast Chronicles, First Five*. Madeira Park: Harbour Publishing.

Leechman, Douglas   1952
"The Nanaimo Petroglyph." *Canadian Geographical Journal*, V. 44, June.

Mallery, Garrick   1972
*Picture-Writing of the American Indians*. New York: Dover Publications.

Meade, Ed   1971
*Indian Rock Carvings of the Pacific Northwest*. Sidney: Gray's Publishing.

McClure, Richard Jr.   1979
*Dating Petroglyphs and Pictographs in Washington*. Olympia: The Evergreen State College.

McClure, Richard Jr.   1980
"The Archawat Petroglyphs and Nootkan Mythology." *CRARA Newsletter*, no. 14.

McFeat, Tom   1966
*Indians of the North Pacific*. Seattle: McClelland & Stewart.

Newcombe, C. F.   1907
"Petroglyphs in B.C." *Victoria Daily Times*, September 7.

Stewart, Hilary   1977
*Indian Fishing. Early Methods on the Northwest Coast*. North Vancouver: J. J. Douglas.

Vastokas, Joan and Vastokas, Romas   1973
*Sacred Art of the Algonkians*. Peterborough: Mansard Press.

# INDEX

111